Paved With Gold, Indeed!

A collection of poems which reflect my experience of life in the City of London

Poems by
Grant Hills

These illustrations reflect my interpretation of Grant's unique insight into the London insurance market

Illustrations by
Sam Burnard

Published by Grant Hills in 2017

Copyright ©Grant Hills 2017

Illustrations by Sam Burnard

Printed by
Dolman Scott ltd
www.dolmanscott.co.uk

Contents

Foreword

This book of poems is a little gem. A timeless
pocket guide to all you wanted to know about the
London insurance market over the years, written with
a wonderful wit and humour by someone who has
experienced it all. The poems effortlessly knit together
all of the goings on in the market, its origins and its
peculiarities, which will inform as well as humour the
reader. The beauty of the book is that you can dip in
and out of the poems at your leisure, in whatever order
you like. Give this little book just a few moments of
your time and you'll feel rewarded, and what's more
because the profits from sale go to charity, you can
feel good in the knowledge that you'll have brightened
someone else's day.

Seen through the eyes of one of the Lloyd's market's
much loved practitioners, Grant Hills shares his
experiences and takes the reader on a light-hearted
stroll through the old and the new of the Lloyd's
Market, the buildings, it's people and some of the
curious oddities that have shaped the market we see
today. Grant's natural warmth and charm shine through
in his colourful and vivid poetic recollections of the
market. The book is an absolute joy and a gift to us all.
Enjoy!

Neil Owen

The Author's Story

"I am not really sure what I can suggest to you!,
Qualifications and talents you have but a few",
Such fond memories of that Careers Master of mine,
Can't remember his name because of the sands of time.
It was with this lack of confidence that off I did set,
A job in The City was my new aim to get.

The ACME Agency was such a marvellous place,
Cards with vacancies "We will find you a space,
Here is one that will fit with you young man",
Aviation Claims and new horizons did span.
The years flew by and my knowledge did grow,
I took off, set up a Claims Department, don't you know!

Hurricanes did blow and the claims they did come,
It was all quite hard work, but we had lots of fun.
How I loved being in charge of that Claims Mob,
"The spiral killed the business," you could hear them sob.
No matter to me, for it was time to move to another place,
Back into casualty business was to be my new space.

My time in this market has been good to me,
A great opportunity and that's clear to see.
Lots of nice people and some great days out,
"It's all about networking" came the loud shout.
What a fabulous market and so full of history,
A soft market is hard.... now that's a mystery.

The Bank Account

Leaving Eltham College to start a new life stage,
A bank account was required to deposit my wage.
I was sent across the road to the Midland Bank,
Where with a single request my heart, it sank,
"Please put your signature just here and there,"
"I don't have one" I said with a voice full of fear.
I tried at first, to simply print my name,
"That won't do!".... oh how I felt the shame!
I finally got one down that had a nice look,
And with that they sent me my first cheque book.

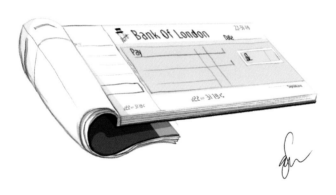

Churches

In the old London walls of our dear City,
Were 'over 100' Church spires and oh so pretty.
But that was before the great fire of 1666,
So Sir Christopher Wren was commissioned to fix.
The flames from the fire destroyed 89 overall,
But the acts of 1670 said rebuild 51, some quite tall.

The Churches are still in the Square Mile abound,
Stroll round The City and they are easily found.
Nestled between the buildings, both old and new,
Over the years I have only been in a few.
Sometimes in The City financial problems we share,
It helps to have a Church to make a small prayer.

Pubs, Restaurants and Wine Bars

Lunch in The City is such a jolly affair,
Wine bars, pubs and restaurants all so near.
A chance to relax and have a glass or two,
Meet up with friends and make acquaintances new.
The days of the long lunch seem now far away,
There lay some tales to be told another day.

Stroll down Cornhill and left into a small alleyway,
Simpsons Tavern, opened in 1757, still the same today.
The finest tradition for good food, ale and wine,
A taste of old London in this fastfood time.
If you prefer the more modern places to eat,
There are plenty of places you can still book a seat.

And so to a few pubs we enjoy in the old Square Mile,
The New Moon & The East India Arms to stay for a while.
The Swan Tavern crosses over the path below,
The Cock & Woolpack and The Jamaica, good places to go.
But there is one pub many City folk may think best of its kind,
The Lamb in Leadenhall Market, full of folk of like mind.

The wine bars in The City are both modern and old,
And some of the starting prices are a little too bold.
But the blend and the choice provides something for all,
From The Gherkin to The Planet of the Grapes in Leadenhall.
Take a stroll down Artillery Lane and The Grapeshots you find,
Full of character and charm in a world left behind.

9

The Placing Broker

The Broker's role is tricky and one to muse,
Bring together Client and Market then try to fuse.
A person, who of the answer must,
Be knowledgeable and honest to build their trust.
Work and play are done with equal zest,
Never disagree with the Client.... even in jest.

Networking he does we should not underestimate,
Nor his expertise to help calculate the correct rate.
The cut of his suit and of the swanky new tie,
He will do all to charm with a blink of an eye.
Winning new Clients is his bread and butter,
When he loses: "you win some and lose some", he will mutter.

The Market he works in may well have moved on,
Quill pens, dusty ledgers from an era bygone.
Regulators, computers, metrics and that kind of stuff,
Makes the Broker huff and puff.
But the thing that makes London such a great place to be,
It blends its history and culture and that is clear to see.

Electronic trading, the boffins do say,
Is essential, saves costs and is here to stay.
Cut out the Broker and the Market will fade,
Lloyd's will fall quickly into the shade.
Work out the fine balance to bring the two together,
And who knows the Old Market might be here forever?

The Bank of England

In the most majestic part of our City,
Sits a building so grand and pretty,
Known as the Old Lady of Threadneedle Street,
The Bank of England, an architectural feat.

Founded in 1694 as a central bank,
A Scotsman, William Paterson, we have to thank,
He noticed our finances were in disarray,
And set up a system for subscribers to pay.

A great thing to do and a bit of a treat,
The free-to-enter museum is very neat,
Balance the Economy or pick up the gold bar,
It's next to Bank Tube Station and not too far.

The Claims Broker

The Claims Broker's role is to get losses agreed,
With the various Syndicates and Companies we cede.
The knowledge of the policy and details of the claim,
Guide the Adjuster and obtain agreement the aim.
Answer any questions that may get thrown at them,
If you don't know your files they will soon condemn.

The Insurance Market was full of these folk,
Waiting with their files in rooms full of smoke.
Back in the day with no rules on behaviour,
Building some respect was your only real saviour.
Sometimes the anger of the Adjuster could grow,
Bad presentation and out the window the file would go.

Now time has passed and things have moved on,
Computers are where we do our business from.
No need for an army of Claims Brokers around,
There are less and less of their kind to be found.
For electronic claims adjusting is now fully in place,
Claims Advocates, most knowledgable now fill that space.

The Human Resources Department

Every company has to have one,
To ensure Company fair play is always done.
They are there for all your troubles and woe,
And to make sure you are paid your company dough.
They may not really know the business you do,
But will try to ensure fair play and look after you.

The Claims Adjuster

To view the claims and make sure they attach,
The loss that is shown which needs a 'Scratch'
The Scratch is a term that indicates it was seen,
By the Claims Adjuster, who is not always keen.
For too many claims is not always that great,
But on the plus side it will improve next year's rate.

The Broker puts forward all the vital information,
In the hope that the Adjuster gives his confirmation.
But the Adjuster knows the Broker's subtle style,
And ponders all the details for quite a while.
With the claims agreed and all business done,
The talk turns to other matters and things more fun.

Goldfinger

My early days in Lloyd's were quite a "scare",
Match Syndicate and "Box Numbers" then broke with fear.
For stories of having your claim declined and thrown out,
"Have you read this file!", the Adjuster would shout.
I was told of one most dastardly tale,
Of a file thrown from the window when the Broker did fail.

There was one sight that I would watch quite in awe,
A man they called Goldfinger they all queued for.
Not wanting to hear what the Placing Broker would tell,
For he would decide yes or no without the hard sell.
Risk then written or declined in the blink of an eye,
Then on to the next Broker, for it was his turn to try.

Lloyd's of London

You may well ask how Lloyd's came about,
With Characters of the day so portly and stout.
It all began in a coffee house in Tower Street,
Where gentlemen coffee drinkers daily would meet.
A reward of a guinea for stolen watches was made,
Edward Lloyd's coffee house, where you would get paid.

Time strolled on and a reputation did grow,
And it slowly became the place for Insurance to go.
Merchants with ships transporting goods far & wide,
Businessmen with wealth to insure for the ride.
But if you were a person with friendships all-round,
You were the Broker bringing parties together and bound.

Leaving the coffee houses to a more permanent place,
The Royal Exchange, backed by subscribers Lloyd's did race.
And even though Edward had died many years before,
His name was kept and proudly hung over the door.
Another move and away from the Royal Exchange,
Located in Leadenhall Street by way of a change.

Across the road in 1958 did Lloyd's move away,
And that is the site that now Willis does stay.
Trading did boom and 1986 a move was once more,
A modern new structure into the skyline did soar.
And here it stays housing the famous Lutine Bell,
But how long it stays here no-one can tell.

First Lady of Lloyd's

Liliana Archibald was the first lady Broker in the Room,
The gentleman gathered around and their eyes did zoom.
A glimpse of the lady with the flame coloured hair,
And now this moment in history they did share.
Liliana then went on to become a Lloyd's Name,
Another first but now with a share of risk in the game.
"I did not break down the barriers" she did say,
"They were broken down for me by the members of Lloyd's
 In a very charming way."

The Lutine Bell

The French did first own the Lutine Bell,
But into the arms of the Royal Navy it fell.
HMS Lutine, a fifth-rate frigate with 38 guns,
She served as an escort on many Dutch runs.

In October of 1799, filled with gold bullion and coin,
Lutine sank in a gale and other wrecks did she join.
All but one of the passengers and crew did die,
With all that gold lost in but a blink of an eye.

In the July of the year 1858 the Bell was found,
Lloyd's, at The Royal Exchange, it would now sound.
Once for bad news and two for good, it was rung,
Fair trade for all and stop traders being stung.

The Bell holds its place in Lloyd's still to this day,
A symbol of this great institution, I have to say.
Now we do not hear its sound quite so much,
But if you do, your heart it will touch.

Leadenhall Market

Leadenhall Market is the most amazing place;
A rich history going back and one we should trace.
A Roman basilica and forum in the heart of our City,
Then Sir Hugh Neville's mansion, and oh so pretty.
Dick Whittington, the Mayor, gave it to the Corporation,
Where it remains in good care for all our admiration.

It was a granary with schools, and a chapel there too,
Trade in wool, linen and metal objects to name just a few.
In 1418, the building was severely damaged by fire,
But rebuilt soon after for all visitors to admire.
The Great Fire of London in 1666,
Burnt the Market but again they did fix.

The Market is placed in a high point of the Square Mile,
Water got pumped from the Thames; quite a trial.
From there gravity does its very own thing,
Water to the whole of the City it did bring.
Leadenhall is truly a very magical place to be,
Harry Potter's Diagon Alley is here to see.

Remaining vibrant and diverse as this poem is told,
Shops, restaurants, events and characters to behold.
I am sure that the Market will continue just to be,
A place that will be enjoyed and for visitors to see.
If Dick Whittington and his cat could see it today,
Might his words be: "Not paved in gold but here to stay."

Tea Ladies

The clatter of the tea trolley coming your way,
A joyous break from processing claims, I say.
"Do you fancy some sugar or are you sweet enough?"
"No, but I will have a Chairman's biscuit or a cheese puff,"
"You cheeky little tyke," she said as she went on her way,
And guess what....? she put salt in my tea the very next day.
With this little poem I send my appreciation,
To Betty, Joyce and Vi, this little dedication.

Dress Code in The City

Over the years, the dress code has moved on,
From long-tail coats and cravats they did don.
Now with the more modern suit worn today,
"It's standards you know" and that's what we say.
But, my friends, there is a wind of change out there,
It's called 'dress down' and who knows what they'll wear?

The Slip

The document to indicate your participation,
A Broker-made slip and quite a creation.
Once your mark is signed upon the slip,
You might upon loss have pockets to dip.
But this slip is different, for it is just to show,
Generosity by you and to charity it will go.

Slip

Prince's Trust

Raising funds to support
The Prince's Trust

Broker	Grant Hills
Type of Cover	Helping to give young people an opportunity
Period	2017
Charity	The Prince's Trust

Twin Towers

The two towers rose into the morning sky,
Symbols of unity, progression, success.
People from all cultures working together,
Another day in this fantastic eclectic place.

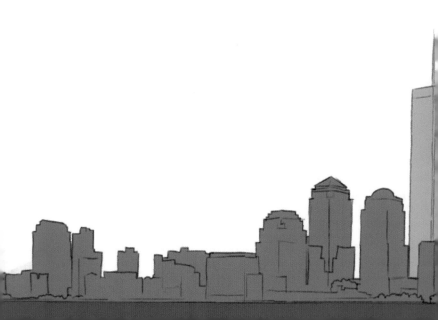

The sunlight which shone that morning,
Was the last they ever saw.
"Then the World shook twice,
May their souls rest in peace."

A Royal Visit

Prince Charles came to Lloyd's and a tour did he take,
Of our new building and a few hands he did shake,
He did spy us in a small group of just about three,
He came over and oh Lord! One of those people was me!
We chatted and smiled and talked of glass lifts.
The Chairman of Lloyd's made some quite awkward shifts,
As the Prince did move on to the official meeting places,
We tried hard but failed, to wipe smiles from our faces.

The Illustrator

With the poems written some time back,
There was an ingredient missing to get on track.
For there was still something that they required,
If I was to produce a book to which I aspired.
To bring them to life I needed an Illustrator,
Characters, buildings, atmosphere.... a creator.

It happened by chance on a Boxing Day,
My niece's new boyfriend joined the melee.
"So what job would you like, may I ask?"
"A Designer or an Illustrator" he said and I did gasp,
"I think I have just the project for you,"
Sam Burnard set straight about drawing a few.

The book now complete for all to read,
And raising some money for those in need.
Simply my memories of the Square Mile,
Sam's interpretations in picture to bring a smile.
We both hope you enjoy the few little rhymes,
With illustrations reflecting some bygone times.

Christmas in The City

Christmas in the City has always been a fun time,
Fir trees shipped in, decorated and looking quite fine.
Cocktail parties, office gatherings and happy times had,
So what has changed since I was a young lad?
Children coming to our offices in their droves,
All dressed to the nines in brand new clothes.

I seem to remember being at the start of that trend,
Bringing just one, but there were three by the end.
There was Charlotte then Claire and finally our Steph,
The excitement beforehand could have made you quite deaf.
A few chocolates and playing with the binding machine,
Now it's full entertainment with animals, I have seen!

The cards may have gone and e-messages fill their place,
In this fast-moving World that fills our space.
But the charm of The City in that magical time,
Will continue to change and that's just fine.
For that is as it is and always will be,
If you haven't yet come, you really should see.

Personal Lines

As children, Dad used to come home and tell us about his day in The City, The poems in this book brought these childhood memories back to life.

For Dad, the City is a whole world in itself, and is one that's constantly evolving. We love that he's captured some of it's unique places, quirks and characters for others to see and meet too.

We are extremely proud of Dad for creating 'Paved With Gold, Indeed', and for making the most of the opportunities The City offered him when he started out.

Through the Prince's Trust, it's incredible to think that his book may offer opportunities to other young people beginning their own career journeys.

Charlotte, Claire & Stephanie Hills

Map of The City

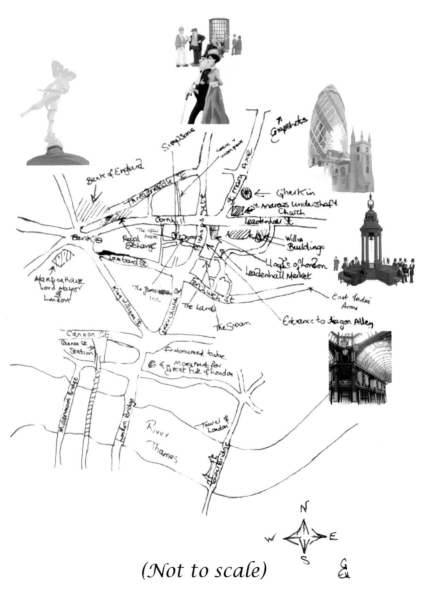

(Not to scale)

It is with Thanks

When I set about producing this book I thought it would be relatively straightforward. I had written a number of the poems a couple of years back and recently found a young talented artist looking to establish himself as an Illustrator. So all I needed was for a few of my friends from London Market to agree to hand over some cash for charity on behalf of their Companies, find a deserving cause, print the book and sell a few........job done. It has been a lot harder than I first imagined and I would like to say thank you to the following people who have helped to make this dream become a reality.

<u>Sponsors</u>

Willis Re
Liberty Specialty Markets
MS Amlin
Ren Re
Brit Syndicates
Trans Re
John Cavanagh – Independent
Andrew Newman – Independent
David Thomas - Independent

Raising funds to support
The Prince's Trust

Prince's Trust

All net proceeds donated to The Prince's Trust.
A registered charity, incorporated by Royal Charter, in England and Wales (1079675) and Scotland (SCO41198).

Inspiration

Lynda Hills
Charlotte Hills
Claire Hills
Stephanie Hills

Logo

Nicky Bruce

Prototype Book

Steven Everitt

Introducers

Adrian Britten
Andy Gaudencio
Dave Stuart
Ella Passingham
Geale Whyte
Jo Williams
Mark Johnson
Steve Harlow
Phil Godwin
Neil Owen
Paul Dunne
Peter McLoughlin

Illustrations and
Book Layout

Sam Burnard

Publishing Advice

John Preston

Foreword

Neil Owen

Proof Readers

Ian Passingham
William Cooper- Rendu
Lauren Kidd
Lynda Hills
Nick Murphy
Joan Bartlett

Personal Lines

Charlotte Hills
Claire Hills
Stephanie Hills

You can find more of Sam's work on his website:
samburnard.com